THE GOLDILOCKS MANIFESTO

How to Govern "Just Right"

Rick Raddatz

The Goldilocks Revolution
7220 W. Jefferson Ave STE 200
Lakewood, CO 80235

Goldilocks.org

eBook, First Edition, November 2024

Cover design by Rick Raddatz

The point of philosophy is to start with something so simple as not to seem worth stating, and to end with something so paradoxical that no one will believe it.

—Bertrand Russell

TABLE OF CONTENTS

PREFACE

When it comes to politics, we the people do not agree on much. But can we agree on the following three things?

1. If we govern too much, that is tyranny.

2. If we govern too little, that is anarchy.

3. If we govern just right, that is ideal.

The challenge, of course, is figuring out what it means to govern "just right." Well, that is what this book is about.

As we pursue this ideal, we will discover the Goldilocks Principle—the guiding principle that helps us know if we are governing too much, too little, or just right.

And here is the good news: There are reasons to believe the Goldilocks Principle is something we can all eventually agree on, healing our political divide in a meaningful way.

So, please enjoy and share this book. That is how you can help change the world. And please join us for our weekly meetings at Goldilocks.org/WeeklyMeeting.

THE STORY OF THE DISCOVERY

It all began Tuesday, November 7th, 2006.

I was sitting on my sofa, eating popcorn, and watching the election results.

Then it happened.

The insanity of our political divide overwhelmed me. I could not take it anymore. In that moment, I knew that I could not sit on the sidelines anymore. I felt called to get involved. I felt called to do something.

But what can one person do?

At first, I considered becoming an activist, a columnist, a blogger, a candidate, or even a radio talk-show host. But the world already had plenty of those kinds of people representing all major viewpoints.

I wanted to make a difference. So, I asked myself a question:

What does the world need?

The answer seemed obvious: *The world needs a breakthrough.*

I came to that conclusion because when people have different political views, there is no way to know who is right. It is all a matter of opinion. A definitive solution would clearly require a breakthrough.

So, I gave myself a mission: *Discover the truth.*

My approach was simple. I put my employees in charge of my small business to free up my time and then I went out full time to talk to strangers.

Talking to strangers about politics turned out to be surprisingly easy.

I would catch a stranger's eye at the airport or a coffee shop and ask with a knowing smile, "So, what do you think about politics?"

Typically, they would laugh and then proceed to share their political views.

At first, I was surprised people were so willing to discuss their political views with a stranger. But later, I came to realize the fact I was a stranger made it easier for them. They could not always be honest with their co-workers, extended family, certain friends, or—sometimes—their spouse or kids. Heck, some people cannot always be honest about their political views with their therapist because they might want to see their therapist again.

But, with a temporary stranger, the floodgates opened, and their political views poured out.

I had thousands of such conversations over the years with people from all points of view—right, left, and center—and all walks of life—from homeless people to billionaires.

As I mentioned, my goal was to make a breakthrough. However, one cannot plan or expect a breakthrough; all one can do is go for it and hope for it to happen.

Two and a half years later, I made the first breakthrough. Five years in, I made the big breakthrough. Then, I spent seven years consulting with hundreds of PhDs to refine the breakthrough and turn it into a proof. Then, I spent five additional years simplifying the proof and learning how best to teach it.

That is how the "Goldilocks Principle" was born.

As a side note, all along this journey, people kept wishing me "Good luck."

Some wished me good luck because they meant it. *Good luck* with that! Some wished me good luck because they thought the task was impossible. Good luck with *that*!

But now the ball is effectively in your court. I still have a role to play, but I cannot change the world on my own. Changing the world will require you and people like you to take the time to get it and share it.

This gives me the perfect opportunity to return the favor and say those two little words to you with all the love in my heart and all the wisdom of the universe:

"Good luck."

THE PROBLEM

At first glance, bringing people together from the right, left, and center in a meaningful way seems impossible. There are just too many issues, too many opinions, too many "facts" and too many opinions about those facts. And since everyone is entitled to their own opinions, it is not clear what can be done.

Human society might be the most complex machine we have ever created. After all, there are 8 billion moving parts—and that is just counting the people. That does not include all the different groups we form, the diverse beliefs we hold, or the technologies we invent, nor the countless goals, issues, and conflicts that exist.

One way to simplify is to group our problems into categories.

First, we have the big problems. These are easy to identify because there is typically an army of PhDs working on them. Yet even the PhDs do not agree on the solution to any of these big problems. Our inability to solve these big problems even with the help of an army of PhDs makes the idea of healing our political divide seem impossible.

Second, we have the small problems—the countless everyday issues that do not have an army of PhDs working on them. The sheer number of these problems is mind-boggling. We cannot even count them. And if we cannot even count them, how could we possibly solve them? Healing our divide seems impossible once again.

Finally, we have future problems – challenges we cannot foresee. For example, new technologies often create new problems. We cannot predict these new technologies and so we cannot predict the problems. So, yet again, healing our political divide seems impossible.

And it gets worse! Not only do we need to solve all the big problems, small problems, and future problems, but need to do so in a way that appeals to the entire political spectrum, is simple enough for everyone to understand, and yet sophisticated enough to earn the respect of the PhDs.

Good luck!

It gets even worse because we live in an age where convincing anyone of anything seems beyond impossible, no matter how logical the argument is.

And finally, there is the problem of dislodging the people and parties in power. People with political power cannot afford to support bold new ideas unless their base already supports it.

For all these reasons, and probably more, it feels like healing our political divide in any meaningful way is a task far beyond our reach.

But there is a trick ... a trick that leads to a solution.

THE SOLUTION

The trick to solving all these seemingly impossible-to-solve problems in a way the right, left, and center can all agree on is to ignore the problems and focus on *incentives*.

You see, we can never know the right answer to any of the problems listed in the previous section, *but we can know the right way to fix incentives.* And if we fix the incentives, we accelerate progress on *all* our problems, earning the support of the entire political spectrum.

So, how do we fix incentives?

Well, it is as simple as the story of Goldilocks.

Consider the following three-step argument that follows the pattern from the story of Goldilocks. It is the same pattern I introduced in the preface, but this time, we will focus on incentives:

1. If we govern too little, we are allowing people to cause harm and that *encourages* people to cause harm. That is clearly a bad incentive.

2. If we govern too much, we become a dictator, forcing our answers onto other people. That kind of concentrated power

encourages the forces of corruption, evil, and money to fight for control of government—another bad incentive.

3. However, if we govern just right (the Goldilocks Government) we minimize harm and do nothing more, nothing less. This allows people the freedom to negotiate. And in that negotiation, people are encouraged to consider the needs and desires of others. Now, *that* is a good incentive, and it is an incentive that accelerates progress.

Aha!

The inescapable conclusion is that the ONLY way to fix incentives is the Goldilocks Principle, which says: "We should govern by minimizing harm. Nothing more. Nothing less."

Please remember that we are not trying to figure out the solution to every problem. We are just focusing on incentives. What we can know for sure is that if we govern too much, we get bad incentives; if we govern too little, we get bad incentives; and it is only when we govern just right—by minimizing harm—that we get good incentives.

A WIN-WIN-WIN

The Goldilocks Principle ends up being a win-win-win—a win for the right, the left, and the center.

If you are a freedom lover on the political right, the Goldilocks Principle offers you maximum freedom, meaning freedom from harm and freedom to act.

If you are a justice lover on the political left, the Goldilocks Principle offers you maximum progress towards an ever-better world—which is the only way to truly maximize justice. After all, there is no way to leap to the perfect world. That would require us to have all the right answers in advance. So. The Goldilocks Principle is the ONLY way to maximize justice.

If you are in the political center, the Goldilocks Principle offers you the fiscally conservative, socially progressive combination you have been waiting for.

So, the Goldilocks Principle offers something for everyone.

Could healing our political divide really be this simple?

Well ... there is one more detail we must add.

We must apply the Goldilocks Principle to the governing of all five types of human action, not just some types of human action.

That is the mistake people made centuries ago.

THE CENTURIES-OLD MISTAKE

The Goldilocks Principle is not new. It was discovered centuries ago by freedom lovers.

But when freedom lovers tried to apply the Goldilocks Principle to the real world, they only applied it to three of the five types of human action (private action, political action, and foreign action). They missed public action and governing action.

Centuries later, this lack of completeness explains the crazy, mixed-up world we live in today.

Think about it ... What kind of society would you expect to have centuries later if the ideal governing principle (the Goldilocks Principle) was only applied three out of five times?

Well, centuries later, you would expect society to be amazing in some ways because we are governing correctly in some ways, accelerating three of the five types of progress. But at the same time, you would expect society to be broken in other ways because we are governing poorly in those other ways, creating bad incentives and not accelerating progress.

And that is exactly the society we live in today.

In fact, the incomplete application of the Goldilocks Principle is why we have the political divide we have today.

You see, the political right sees (correctly) how awesome freedom and limited government are, and so they are SURE they are correct about freedom and limited government.

Meanwhile, the political left sees (correctly) how broken/unjust some parts of society are and so they are SURE they are correct that more needs to be done.

And the center sees (correctly) that both sides have a point and so they are SURE the right answer is some sort of combination.

So, everyone is partially correct ... but nobody is fully correct. And yet, everyone is so SURE they are right. As a result, we have spent centuries fighting each other, blaming each other, and vilifying each other.

What a tragic waste of centuries!

But now, finally, we have the correct answer.

THE CORRECT ANSWER

The correct answer is to apply the Goldilocks Principle to all five types of human action, so we get ALL forms of freedom and ALL forms of progress, maximizing the good in EVERY way, addressing ALL our problems, healing our divide in the process.

Here are the five types of human action again, with a bit more detail:

1. Private action—people going about their private lives

2. Public action—public spending

3. Political action—people running for office

4. Foreign action—anything a foreign power might do

5. Governing action—the attempt to govern all this action

These five types of human action are not controversial. We see them on the news every day. And since all five types of human action can cause harm, we now know the correct answer is to apply the Goldilocks Principle to all five.

PROVING THE TYPES OF ACTION

There is a simple way to prove these five types of action are the correct five and that together, they form a complete set.

Consider the following six-step argument:

1. If there is one person in the world, they can do private action

2. If there are two people in the world, they can pool their resources and have a public budget—public action

3. If there are three people in the world, two can out-vote one, creating political pressure—political action

4. If a fourth person is outside society, that is foreign action from the point of view of that society

5. If we can even conceive of a future person—and we can—there is a question as to how we should govern ourselves in the moment—governing action

6. And finally, if we add more people to this thought experiment and we exhaustively analyze all the combinations, permutations, and points of view, we do not discover any additional types of human action

So those are the five fundamental types of human action—private, public, political, foreign, and governing. Together, they form a complete set, representing ALL human action from the point of view of any one society.

I call this thought experiment "The Genesis Experiment" because it roughly follows the story of Adam and Eve from the book of Genesis in the Bible.

GOVERNING THE FIVE TYPES OF HUMAN ACTION

The correct answer, again, is to apply the Goldilocks Principle to all five types of human action.

It seems so simple, so obvious. And yet, that is not what we are doing right now. Right now, we are only applying the Goldilocks Principle to three of the five types of human action.

The three types of human action we are governing correctly include:

1. Private action—we police private action to minimize harm (theft), establishing economic freedom and creating the incentive for private actors to negotiate. We call it the private economy.

2. Political action—we check-and-balance political action to minimize harm (oppression), establishing political freedom and creating the incentive for political actors to negotiate. We call it the political economy.

3. Foreign action—we defend our nation to minimize harm (invasion), establishing national freedom (freedom as a nation) and cresting the incentive for foreign powers to negotiate. We call it diplomacy.

The two types of human action we are governing incorrectly include:

1. Public action—to minimize the harm (waste) in a public budget, we should be constantly re-prioritizing. Here in the United States, we do that with some of our budgets, but the glaring exception is "entitlement spending," also known as "social spending."

Entitlement spending is dictated spending. Past generations have dictated entitlement promises to future generations. Our generation is stuck in the middle and we do not dare propose changes. Proposing changes to entitlement spending is political suicide. And that is a problem because the only way to improve that spending (helping people better) would be to constantly re-prioritize it.

The people who are harmed are—tragically—the people who need help most in society. No wonder social justice is a major issue!

2. Governing action—The way to minimize the harm of government is to educate the people about the Goldilocks Principle and how it must be applied all five times. But we have never known that the Goldilocks Principle was

supposed to be applied to public action or governing action, and so we have never been able to teach the people the full truth. Correcting this root problem is what the Goldilocks Revolution is all about.

WHAT WE MUST DO

To correct this situation, we must educate a healthy majority of people about the Goldilocks Principle and how to apply it. This gives us a three-step plan to accelerate progress in every way, healing our political divide in the process:

Step 1: Teach people the Goldilocks Principle and how to apply it.

Step 2: Use the Goldilocks Principle to fix all fundamental incentives.

Step 3: Sit back and relax as the people who care argue it all out.

Please note that this plan does not require us to agree on everything. In fact, it only asks us to agree on the Goldilocks Principle. For example, this plan does not ask us to agree on abortion policy, gun control, border security—or any other issue! Instead, the Goldilocks Principle gives us the freedom to disagree about almost everything if only we come together on the Goldilocks Principle itself.

We can now imagine a future where we can sit back and relax while making progress in every way thanks to the widespread acceptance and application of the Goldilocks Principle.

SITTING BACK AND RELAXING?

The idea of sitting back and relaxing (step 3, above) might seem unrealistic but that becomes possible if we get the fundamental incentives right.

For example, when it comes to the private economy, do we have to become experts in iPhone design? Do we need to organize protests to get a better iPhone next year? Do we need to riot in the streets to call attention to the lack of progress with iPhone design?

No.

When it comes to iPhone design—or any product or service the private economy produces—we can all sit back and relax. We can trust economic incentives to make things better and better over time.

If we fix the incentives regarding all five types of human action, that is when we can expect to accelerate progress in every way, and that is when we can finally sit back and relax.

That is not to say we do not have to worry about things like sustainability, but sustainability is one of those issues we will have to argue about forever. The Goldilocks Principle will help us because the only way to de-politicize sustainability is to create a world where we can all sit back and relax on almost every other issue.

CONCLUSION

So, there we go. The Goldilocks Principle applied to all five types of human action does everything we could hope for. It maximizes freedom. It maximizes incentives. It maximizes progress. And therefore, it maximizes justice.

To propose ANY other solution is to either govern too much, govern too little, or a combination of both.

THE FLOW CHART

The following flowchart might help you visualize everything we have discussed. Each of the boxes is numbered for easy reference.

1. If we govern too much, that is tyranny (boxes 1 and 2)

2. If we govern too little, that is anarchy (boxes 3 and 4)

3. If we govern just right, we get freedom and good incentives (boxes 5, 6, and 7)

4. Good incentives maximize progress and—over time—justice (boxes 8 and 9)

5. We must remember to apply the Goldilocks Principle to all five types of human action—private, public, political, foreign, and governing (box 10)

HOW SHOULD WE GOVERN?

(1) TOO MUCH (CAUSE HARM) → (2) TYRANNY

(3) TOO LITTLE (ALLOW HARM) → (4) ANARCHY

(5) JUST RIGHT (MINIMIZE HARM) → (6) FREEDOM and (7) INCENTIVES

(7) INCENTIVES → (8) PROGRESS → (9) JUSTICE

(10) We must apply this to all five types of action: PRIVATE, PUBLIC, POLITICAL, FOREIGN, and GOVERNING.

THE GOLDILOCKS REVOLUTION

BATTERED VOTER SYNDROME

Some people who hear the solution say, "That is a well-reasoned argument, but the other side does not listen to reason, so there is no hope. It will never happen."

I call this "battered voter syndrome".

These people typically care deeply about the ideological/political war but have lost hope. If this describes you, I have three suggestions:

1. Please check out the hundreds of amazing testimonials on Goldilocks.org from all points of view and realize that there is hope. People from all points of view can get this.

2. Please remember that the rather vocal people you might have had an argument with are not the same as the shyer people who might avoid arguments. So even though reason has failed with everyone you did have an argument with, reason might work on everyone you did not have an argument with.

3. And finally, remember that the power of an argument changes over time as the argument gets more support. Someone who resists your argument today might come

around after they see other people they respect being open to the argument.

In other words, there is hope!!!

THE DANGER

What if we ignore the Goldilocks Principle?

What if we just keep doing what we have been doing?

What is the danger?

Well, let us consider four dangers:

1. Economic collapse
2. Environmental collapse
3. Geopolitical collapse
4. Social-political collapse

ECONOMIC COLLAPSE

In 1950, Venezuela was the fourth wealthiest nation in the world on a per-capita (per-person) basis. A few decades later, Venezuelans were so desperate to feed their families, they were eating zoo animals.

In the early 2000s, Greece was a perfectly pleasant, modern European nation. I even honeymooned there in 2001. But thanks to the 2008-2016 economic collapse, young girls became prostitutes at such an alarming rate (clearly out of desperation) that the price of a prostitute dropped to the price of a sandwich.

Nobody involved wanted that type of collapse in either country. Things just spiraled out of control.

In Venezuela, it happened because of a combination of corruption, socialism, and geopolitical drama. But all three causes have something in common—the left-right political divide fuels all three. How can a country root out corruption if it is hopelessly divided and both sides must do whatever it takes to survive? How can socialism be fought if the forces of economic freedom do not have the right answer to social justice? How can geopolitical drama not happen when a corrupt socialist regime is in power?

In Greece, it also happened because of a combination of corruption, socialism, and geopolitical drama. The details were different, but the result was similar—economic collapse.

If you think that kind of collapse cannot happen here, well, I am sorry, but you are in denial. And once it is obvious that things are out of control, it is already too late—the downward spiral becomes unstoppable.

Conclusion: We need to come together on the Goldilocks Principle NOW

ENVIRONMENTAL COLLAPSE

The thing about the environment is that we do not really know how everything is connected biologically, chemically, or climatically. That means we do not know what the real limits are, and perhaps we never can.

But there are signs we are beyond the limits already. For example, the Earth has experienced five previous mass-extinction events from natural causes, but the current human-induced mass-extinction event is already on par with previous extinction events and, since it is human-caused, it is only going to accelerate unless we get our act together.

That means we need the political will to live within conservative environmental limits. But our inability to live within reasonable fiscal limits is not a good sign.

Think about it. The effects of poor economic policies play out over years and decades, and we know the limits—yet we cannot live within those limits because of our divide. Meanwhile, the effects of poor environmental policies play out over decades and centuries—meaning the problem is harder—and we do not know the limits.

If we cannot get our act together fiscally, how the heck do we expect to get our act together environmentally? Our only hope is to come together on the fundamentals of how best to govern.

Conclusion: We need to come together on the Goldilocks Principle NOW.

GEOPOLITICAL COLLAPSE

We had two world wars in the last century. It is nice to think we ire past that type of thing, but the common theme of this section is that things can spiral out of control even if nobody wants it to.

How might World War III start? Well, there is only one way for it to start. It unavoidably must start with desperate, unstable countries with different philosophical foundations.

Do we currently have desperate, unstable countries with different philosophical foundations?

Yes.

Well, then, we are at risk.

Conclusion: We need to come together on the Goldilocks Principle NOW.

SOCIAL-POLITICAL COLLAPSE

The robot revolution is near. If you think Elon Musk is rich now ... wait until he starts selling human-sized robots that are more capable than humans in almost every way. Version 1 of his robots might not be that ... but version 3?

Think of the social-political impact.

In the past, technological advances have always been a net-positive overall, and any workers displaced had other jobs they could switch to.

But what happens when the robots are better than us at pretty much everything?

Are we all going to become nurses and prostitutes?

I mean, those are the jobs that are most resilient to the robot revolution, right?

I do not know about you, but I am going to stock up on sandwiches!

But seriously, the robot revolution has the potential to either create the best possible world for humans, or the worst possible world—ending humanity's very existence.

Either way, we know one thing for sure: The social upheaval coming in the next few decades will be the greatest social upheaval in human history, and history says we are perfectly capable of screwing it up.

Which future we have in store for us and how well we navigate the transition depends on exactly one thing: coming together on the fundamentals about how best to govern.

Conclusion: We need to come together on the Goldilocks Principle NOW.

A BETTER FUTURE

In the last section, we explored the various forms of collapse that might happen if we fail to spread the word about the Goldilocks Principle.

But what should we expect if we *do* spread the word about the Goldilocks Principle?

Well, imagine a world full of healthy nations, where each nation has a healthy majority of people who understand and believe in the Goldilocks Principle and how to apply it.

That would be a world where every nation is maximizing prosperity, social justice, political maturity, international harmony, and sustainability, all at the same time.

It would literally be the best possible world. I mean, we cannot do any better than constant improvement in every way in every nation. Can we? I do not think so. To do better, we would need to have the ultimate dictator who somehow had all the right answers to everything and somehow had the power to force us to a better situation.

But even then, the dictator would need to hand things over to the Goldilocks Principle to improve even more.

So, one way or another, the widespread acceptance of the Goldilocks Principle is the key to building the best possible world.

The rest of the book will dive deeper, helping you understand the specifics about how to implement the Goldilocks Principle across all five types of human action.

But honestly, that level of detail is not necessary for most people to know.

Consider what is needed to sustain the private economy, or what is needed to sustain checks and balances, or what is needed to sustain a strong national defense. Those are the three ways humanity has properly applied the Goldilocks Principle already.

All that is needed to sustain the Goldilocks Principle is a healthy majority of people who have a vague feeling that the Goldilocks Principle is the right thing to do. The details are not important.

Well, the same thing for the remaining two ways; we need to apply the Goldilocks Principle.

We do not need everyone to become a philosopher or intellectual.

All we need is a healthy majority of people who have a vague feeling that the Goldilocks Principle is the right thing to do in all five ways.

Humanity has already demonstrated that is possible by sustaining a healthy majority of people who have a vague feeling that the Goldilocks Principle is the right thing to do in three of the five ways for centuries.

Now, we just need to do it two more times.

That is it.

It is that simple.

If you make it more complicated than that, then you are not getting the core insight.

The core insight is that we may never agree on all the details, but that is ok. If we can largely agree on the fundamentals ... if we can largely agree on the Goldilocks Principle and that it needs to be applied five times, that is good enough. That is all we need to accelerate progress in every way.

We can never do better than that.

And we CAN do that.

So, let us do that.

I invite you right now to do one of the following:

1. Share Goldilocks.org with your friends and followers

2. Visit Goldilocks.org\volunteer

3. Visit Goldilocks.org\donate

Sharing, volunteering, and donating—that is how we will change the world and make this more perfect vision a reality.

DIVING DEEPER

In the earlier section, I argued that the average voter does not need more details.

But you are not the average voter, are you?

If you are reading this section, I suspect that compared to the average voter, you are more intelligent, more educated, more capable, more influential, and more respected.

So, in this section, we will prepare to apply the Goldilocks Principle to all five types of human action.

To do this, we will convert the flowchart from page 25 into the table on the next page. The various concepts in the flowchart will become column headings. The five types of action will become row headings. And when we fill in the table, we will be applying the Goldilocks Principle to all five types of human action with precision and completeness.

First, let us simplify the concepts in the flowchart.

We can combine boxes 1, 2, 3, and 4 (governing too much, tyranny, governing too little, anarchy) into a single box called "harm."

Likewise, we can combine boxes 7 and 8 (incentives and progress) into a single box called "Negotiation."

Then, let us add a new box called "Sustainability." Being unsustainable is just a special type of harm (harm to future people), but I want to separate it so we do not forget it.

Then, let us separate the five types of action into their own boxes and put them on the left side.

I call this table the "Pentanomic Table" because each row describes how to economize (maximize the good of) a different type of human action. In short, the existence of five types of action means the potential for five economies.

Here is the result:

THE PENTANOMIC TABLE

ACTION	HARM	MIN HARM	FREEDOM	SUSTAINABILITY	NEGOTIATION	MAX GOOD
PRIVATE						
PUBLIC						
POLITICAL						
FOREIGN						
GOVERNING						

In one sense, we have not really changed much. But this new layout creates the space we need to apply the Goldilocks Principle to all five types of human action in the next section.

ALL THE WAY DEEP

In the previous chapter, we transformed the Goldilocks Flow Chart into the table on page 43. At this stage, the table only has row headings (the five types of action) and column headings (the concepts related to the Goldilocks Principle).

Filling in the table is surprisingly simple—we just need to look at how all the row headings and column headings relate.

THE HARM COLUMN

1. Private actors can commit **theft.**

2. Public spending can be a **waste.**

3. Political action can lead to **oppression.**

4. Foreign actors (foreign powers) can cause **invasion.**

5. We can govern too much or too little—**bad government.**

THE MINIMIZE HARM COLUMN

1. We need to **police** private action to minimize theft

2. We need to **prioritize** our public budgets to minimize waste.

3. We need to **check and balance** political ambition to minimize oppression.

4. We need to **defend** our nation to protect against foreign threats like invasion.

5. And we need to **educate** the people on the Goldilocks Principle to ensure we govern just right—not too much, not too little.

THE FREEDOM COLUMN

1. By protecting ourselves against private theft, we achieve **economic freedom.**

2. Prioritizing the budget creates **priority freedom**—the freedom any group of free people should have to prioritize their budget their way.

3. Through checking and balancing political ambition, we get **political freedom**—the freedom to believe whatever we want.

4. Defending the nation provides us with freedom as a nation—**national freedom.**

5. Maintaining a healthy majority of people who believe in the Goldilocks Principle will protect us from harmful ideologies (any ideology that conflicts with the Goldilocks Principle), giving us **ideological freedom.**

Some people confuse political freedom and ideological freedom. Political freedom is the freedom to believe anything. Ideological freedom is when we are educated enough not to believe in ideologies that conflict with the Goldilocks Principle.

THE SUSTAINABILITY COLUMN

1. In the private economy, we must respect the limits of **environmental sustainability.**

2. In the public economy, we need to ensure **fiscal sustainability.**

3. In the political economy, we aim for **political sustainability**, which enforces the right for future generations to vote.

4. In the foreign economy, **geopolitical sustainability** requires that we protect the future from dangerous foreign powers that threaten global peace.

5. Finally, **ideological sustainability** requires that we pass our knowledge of the Goldilocks Principle to the next generation.

THE NEGOTIATION COLUMN

1. In the private economy, we negotiate **prices.**
2. In the public economy, we negotiate **priorities**—what we value more than money!
3. In the political economy, political factions are forced to negotiate real-world **compromises**.
4. In the economy of foreign affairs, we negotiate **trade deals and alliances.**
5. In the governing economy, we negotiate the **ideal justice**—the ideal we strive for

Historical note: In the 1800s, philosopher Karl Marx argued that the prices negotiated in the private economy did not account for the full value of the goods and services being negotiated. Marx was right! It is only by considering all five negotiations that we can understand the full value of anything in society.

THE MAX GOOD COLUMN

Each negotiation includes the incentive to consider the needs and desires of others. This is what leads to constant improvement (progress) on average over time, maximizing the good overall.

1. In the private economy, constant improvement leads to general **prosperity**, though some people may be left behind.

2. In the public economy, constantly re-prioritizing the social spending budget improves our ability to help those who get left behind, maximizing **social justice.**

3. In the political economy, ever better compromises maximize political **maturity.**

4. In the foreign affairs economy, if every nation is properly incentivizing every other nation to negotiate (rather than invading), we are maximizing international **harmony.**

5. And in the governing economy, as we improve governance over time, we are beginning to create the **best future** possible.

We have now filled in the Pentanomic Table. In the next section, we will compare the modern world to this pentanomic ideal.

THE PENTANOMIC TABLE

ACTION	HARM	MIN HARM	FREEDOM	SUSTAINABILITY	NEGOTIATION	MAX GOOD
PRIVATE	THEFT	POLICE	ECONOMIC	ENVIRONMENTAL	PRICES	PROSPERITY
PUBLIC	WASTE	PRIORITIZE	PRIORITY	FISCAL	PRIORITIES	SOCIAL JUSTICE
POLITICAL	OPPRESSION	CHECK & BAL	POLITICAL	POLITICAL	COMPROMISES	MATURITY
FOREIGN	INVASION	DEFEND	NATIONAL	GEO-POLITICAL	ALLIANCES, ETC	HARMONY
GOVERNING	BAD GOVT	EDUCATE	IDEOLOGICAL	IDEOLOGICAL	IDEAL JUSTICE	BEST FUTURE

TODAY VS THE IDEAL

Earlier, we described the ideal world as the following: Imagine a world where every nation is maximizing prosperity, social justice, political maturity, international harmony, and sustainability, all at the same time, thanks to every nation having a healthy majority of people who believe in and support the Goldilocks Principle and how to apply it.

So, how does our world today compare to that ideal?

Well, we are about 3/5ths of the way there.

As discussed earlier, centuries ago, humanity figured out how to properly structure three of the five economies—the private economy, the political economy, and the foreign affairs economy. We can always do better, of course, but at least these three areas are not completely broken.

Some people might say, "Wait a minute, politics IS completely broken!"

But is it?

Are we truly in danger of having a dictator here in the U.S.? Political parties like to scare everyone with such claims, but the truth is that checks and balances are in place and working and both major parties are forced to compromise and those compromises over time tend to improve things.

The truly broken parts of society are: (1) the lack of social justice thanks to a century of entitlement spending (dictated spending) instead of prioritized spending (constantly improving spending) and (2) the weird mix of governing too much and too little (bad government) that we have today thanks to nobody ever discovering the need to apply the Goldilocks Principle to all five types of human action.

Luckily these two problems are easy to solve now that we understand both the problem and the solution so clearly.

For example, the state of Oregon has been prioritizing their Medicaid spending for more than 30 years. That is evidence that it is in fact possible to prioritize our social spending. We just need to find the political will to do it.

Where will we find the political will?

Simple. The political will comes AFTER a healthy majority of people come to believe in and support the Goldilocks Principle and how to apply it.

And the second major problem—getting the government back on track—requires the exact same effort—getting a healthy majority of people come to believe in and support the Goldilocks Principle and how to apply it.

Therefore, the only difference between today's world and the ideal world is the number of people who believe in and support the Goldilocks Principle and how to apply it.

That means we know exactly what must be done. We must help a healthy majority of people in every nation believe in and support the Goldilocks Principle and how to apply it.

SPECIAL TOPICS

There are three topics that need special attention because ignorance on these topics is responsible for almost all our suffering. The three topics are (1) greed, (2) social justice, and (3) the role of opinions.

GREED

Confusion about greed is one of the primary reasons for our political divide. For example, have you ever heard someone say (or have you ever said) that the problem in our society is greedy capitalists or greedy corporations?

This section will resolve this conflict once and for all!

First, let us consider the options for dealing with greed:

1. **Outlaw Greedy Thoughts:** We could outlaw greed by inventing brain scanners and putting anyone with greedy thoughts in jail—but then everyone would be in jail!

2. **Outlaw Greedy Acts:** We could outlaw greedy acts—any act that was done out of greed. But when a business owner lowers prices because he or she greedily wants more market share, we usually welcome that. So outlawing greedy acts does not

seem right.

3. **Force People to Do Good:** We could force greedy people to do whatever those in power believe is good.

   There are three huge problems with this. First, forcing an answer onto society locks in that answer and destroys the potential for progress. Second, it attracts corruption, evil, and money into government—a bad incentive. Third, the laws of economics conspire to hurt exactly the people we are trying to help when we do this.

   A simple example of this last point is the minimum wage. The intention behind a minimum wage is almost always good. But the results are catastrophic.

   You see, establishing a minimum wage makes those jobs more attractive, attracting more and better applicants. But that is a problem because, the people who need help most find it harder to compete against more and better applicants.

   In short, minimum wage, on average, necessarily helps people who need help less (the new applicants) at the expense of people who need help most.

   If someone knowingly hurts the people who need help most, it is evil. If it is done out of ignorance or denial, it is tragic.

4. **Outlaw Harmful Acts:** With this option, we forget greed and focus on harm by outlawing harmful acts—acts that cause harm. That would force greedy people who might otherwise cause harm to negotiate, and that negotiation would force greedy people to consider the needs and desires of others, accelerating progress over time.

5. **Do Nothing:** Or we could do nothing and let greedy people run amok, causing harm. Anarchy!

It should be obvious, but options 1, 2, and 3 are examples of governing too much. Option 5 is governing too little. Option 4 is the Goldilocks Principle—the ideal.

So, what does this mean? It means greed is not the problem. Greed is a fact of life, and we have a fundamental choice. We can govern too much, we can govern too little, or we can govern just right—a la the Goldilocks Principle.

It also means that anyone who complains about greedy capitalists or greedy corporations clearly does not know what they are talking about and should be ignored and/or educated.

In the past, such arguments could be excused because the freedom-loving capitalists did not have an answer to social justice—nobody did. But now we do.

Now we know that the only way to maximize social justice is to apply this same argument to public action (public spending) and maximize the good of public spending so we help the people who need help most in society as best we can. We cannot do better than that.

The key insight here is that the private economy is NOT powered by greed. It is powered by good incentives. And those good incentives work on *everyone*, whether greedy or generous.

There is one more aspect of greed we need to discuss: there are five *types* of greed. This is because there are five types of action. Greed can be expressed via (1) private action, (2) public action, (3) political action, (4) foreign action, and (5) governing action.

The private economy is not powered by greed. It is powered by good incentives.

And that means we can extend our argument about greed to all five spheres, and we can conclude that in no situation is greed the problem. Greed, again, is simply a fact of life and the question is how best to govern.

We have never had this degree of precision or completeness before.

SOCIAL JUSTICE

Confusion about what social justice is and how best to pursue it also lies at the heart of our political divide.

Let us begin with a definition of social justice.

To do so, I propose we focus on the *goal* of social justice rather than any one approach. This makes sense because most people can agree on the goal. It is the approach that we strongly disagree on.

Proposed definition of social justice: Social justice is about helping those who need help most as best we can.

Using this definition, social justice is clearly a good thing. After all, how evil would an individual have to be to *oppose* helping those who need it most? And we cannot do any better than the best we can.

Before we explore the potential approaches, here are a few important points:

- Some of these approaches will help everyone, including the rich, but they are included because they also help those who need help most (our goal). Excluding these approaches to social justice would only force the poor to suffer more.

- Some approaches may benefit the rich MORE than the poor. But if we are serious about our goal—helping those who need help most as best we can—we must include these ideas too.

- Finally, some approaches help poor people at the expense of the rich. This creates a potential ethical dilemma. Luckily, the ethical dilemma is avoided because the approaches in question are ultimately voluntary for those who are funding it, and the voluntary participation makes it ethical.

Without further ado, here are five good ways to pursue social justice and two bad ways:

Good Way #1—Equal Rights: The establishment of equal rights benefits everyone, but it especially helps the poor. By "equal rights," I mean not just legal rights, but also equal dignity, respect, and access to culture, institutions, jobs, and more. Equal rights are fundamental to social justice.

Good Way #2—Economic Freedom: Economic freedom also helps everyone, though some argue it helps the rich more than the poor. However, economic freedom clearly does help poor people. You see, poor people are 30 times richer in a society with economic freedom than in a society without economic freedom. In fact, economic freedom has helped raise more people out of poverty than any other system. So yes, economic freedom is a crucial part of helping those who need help most.

Good Way #3—Friends and Family: Friends and family are often the first and best sources of support for those in need. While they cannot do everything, they often know better than anyone else what kind of help the individual needs and when to pull back. Friends and family play a key role in social justice.

Good Way #4—Charity: Privately-funded charity is voluntary, making it ethically sound. Charities can provide help directly to those who need it most, however privately funded charity will inevitably leave gaps. That is where prioritized public assistance (Good Way #5) comes in.

Good Way #5—Prioritized Public Assistance: Public assistance, when successfully prioritized, has the power to help those who fall through the cracks. Ethically, this must be voluntary, meaning that the people who pay taxes should be free to leave society if they prefer. If taxpayers are here voluntarily, then there are no ethical issues. Prioritizing is essential for two reasons: (1) without prioritization, spending is wasted, and (2) without constant re-prioritization, improvements are not made.

Bad Way #1—Economic Intervention: Free-market economists have long argued that any intervention in the private economy—such as price floors, price ceilings, or mandates—ends up hurting the people that need help most. The analysis of minimum wage from earlier is an example of a price floor. The argument against such intervention is often ignored, denied, or ridiculed by anti-free-market advocates. In the past, that reaction was understandable because we did not know the right way to help those who need help most. But now we do (the five good ways above). So now there is no excuse.

Bad Way #2—Entitlement Spending: Entitlement spending suffers from similar problems. The intention is good, but the impact is bad. The problem with entitlement spending is that it locks in a certain amount of good and prevents a competition of ideas that would have discovered even better ideas in time. As the Goldilocks Principle teaches us, the ONLY way to maximize the good of social spending is constant improvement thanks to constant re-prioritization.

By doing all five good ways and avoiding the two bad ways, we can pursue social justice the right way.

THE ROLE OF OPINIONS

It happens all the time. I will be having a nice conversation with someone about the Goldilocks Principle, and we reach a point of conflict. The conflict usually takes one of the following forms:

"This famous philosopher says X,"

or "That famous economist says X,"

or "Everyone knows X,"

or "I believe strongly in X."

The implication is that since the Goldilocks Principle conflicts with X, the Goldilocks Principle must be wrong.

The problem is that "X" is just a theory—a guess—and the Goldilocks Principle is an eternal truth. Therefore, if there is any conflict, the Goldilocks Principle unavoidably wins, and theory X unavoidably loses.

To see that the Goldilocks Principle really is an eternal truth, consider the following claims:

1. We have no choice about the existence of private action.

2. We have no choice about the existence of public action.

3. We have no choice about the existence of political action.

4. We have no choice about the existence of foreign action.

5. We have no choice about the existence of governing action.

6. If these five types of action exist, so does the potential for five types of the following: harm, the governing (minimizing) of harm, freedom, sustainability, negotiation, and maximum good.

7. If we govern too much, that attracts corruption, evil, and money, and that, on average, is a bad incentive if our goal is to maximize the good.

8. If we govern too little, that encourages harm to run amok and that, on average, is a bad incentive if our goal is to maximize the good.

9. If we govern just right (by minimizing harm), we encourage a negotiation where everyone is encouraged to consider the needs and desires of others, which is a good incentive if our goal is to maximize the good.

These nine claims are not up for debate if you understand the logic and the context, just as the fact that 2+2=4 is not up for debate.

The key takeaway here is that the Goldilocks Principle is not just another theory—it is a logical necessity within the context of a human society. If you can break the logic, great. If not, logic demands that the Goldilocks Principle prevails in any conflict with theory X.

COMMON OBJECTIONS

In the long term, reality always wins.

That is good news for the Goldilocks Revolution, as the Goldilocks Principle is derived from pure deductive logic and is, therefore, necessarily correct. That means the Goldilocks Revolution will eventually succeed. It is just a matter of time.

However, in the short term, there is no way around it. Humans are going to have objections, and we must confront those objections head on.

In this section, I will address important objections I have seen from five distinct groups of people: (1) the political far left; (2) the political far right; (3) regular people; (4) PhDs, and (5) people with high emotional intelligence.

Please keep in mind, however, that every individual is different and so you may have a quite different set of questions, concerns, or objections. That is why we are doing weekly meetings (Goldilocks.org/WeeklyMeeting).

Still, some objections are more common than others, so we will address the more common ones here.

First, the political far left has spent centuries fighting against the right-leaning understanding of freedom and capitalism. However, the Goldilocks Principle supports the right-leaning understanding of freedom and capitalism.

Therefore, a common objection from people on the political far left is that the Goldilocks Principle is nothing more than a centuries-old far-right idea and there is nothing new here.

WRONG!

As I have said several times, centuries ago, the freedom lovers who discovered the Goldilocks Principle made a mistake in that the Goldilocks Principle was only applied to three types of human action instead of all five types of human action.

And what is more, the application of the Goldilocks Principle to public action, as discussed in the earlier section, is the key to finally solving social justice, the iconic far-left goal.

So yes, the Goldilocks Principle itself is not new. What is new is our understanding of how to apply it.

Second, the political far right has spent centuries fighting against the left's approach to social justice. And so, many on the political far right will initially reject the Goldilocks Principle's use in the pursuit of social justice.

One thing for the right to consider is that our society is going to have a public budget no matter what and the Goldilocks Principle simply says that budget should be capped and prioritized. Right-leaning people are in favor of capping and prioritizing the public budget. They just never realized that the result would be a competition of ideas that maximizes social justice.

If you are on the political right, it may also help to think of constantly improving public spending as an ever-better safety net instead of "social justice."

Third, regular people are more familiar with debating specific policy proposals than debating political philosophy. For them, the Goldilocks Principle might seem too conceptual or abstract. And so, a common objection regular people have is that they do not see how this will really make a difference.

In response, I would remind people with this objection that incentives clearly work in the real world, and the Goldilocks Principle is, again, all about fixing incentives. This was discussed in the section entitled, "The Solution."

Fourth, PhDs, on the other hand, have no problem engaging with abstract or conceptual arguments. They will recognize the Goldilocks Principle as John Stewart Mills' "Harm Principle." from 1859. If you google it, you will see that the #1 objection PhDs have to the Harm Principle is that there is no way to know for sure what counts as harm.

The response is simple. The fact that we cannot know what counts as harm only means the Goldilocks Principle cannot reveal any specific answers. But we are not asking the Goldilocks Principle to give specific answers! We are asking the Goldilocks Principle to fix incentives. It is good incentives over time that will induce ever better answers.

A real-world example of this is the private economy, which is powered by the Goldilocks Principle. The laws of economics do not give us specific answers. They do not tell us how to design the iPhone, for example. It is good incentives over time that produced the iPhone.

What is more, we have never governed the private economy perfectly. And yet, the private economy, thanks to good incentives, constantly improves products, services and living standards.

By extension, we can conclude we do not have to govern any of the five economies perfectly to expect constant improvement on average in every way, maximizing the good in every way over time. So, we do not need to know nor agree as to what counts as harm. The objection collapses.

Fifth and finally, people who have a high emotional intelligence often complain that they "do not see the humanity" in the Goldilocks argument.

In response, please remember that the Goldilocks Principle only fixes incentives. Once the incentives are improved, the ensuing debate is 100% human vs human as we all express our hopes, dreams, fears, and beliefs. So, it is in that debate that we will see humanity.

To complain that the Goldilocks Principle itself is devoid of humanity is like complaining that math is devoid of humanity— the complaint is completely beside the point.

If you have a different question, concern, or objection, please join us for our weekly live Q&A discussions at Goldilocks.org/WeeklyMeeting.

THE TALKING DOG

In the 2009 Pixar movie, "Up", an old man and a young boy go on an adventure and run into a stray dog who happens to be a talking dog.

The dog is super cute and quite loving, saying, "I just met you, but I love you."

The boy says, "Can we keep him?"

The old man says definitively, "No."

The boy whines, "But he is a talking dog!!!"

That is funny because if you come across a stray talking dog, you keep him. You at least think about it. But the old man's answer was a definitive "No."

Why am I telling you this? I am telling you this because the Goldilocks Principle and the discovery of how to properly apply it is a talking dog. It is a breakthrough. It changes everything. And yet one of the most common responses people have is to treat it as nothing special—as just another proposal.

For the sake of billions of people in the world, do not do that.

The political right and political left have spent centuries fighting for freedom and social justice respectively. They have vilified each other. Wars have been fought. More than a hundred million people have died as a result, either in wars or politically induced famines.

But now we have the solution. Now we know the Goldilocks Principle and how to apply it.

As discussed earlier, if we do not spread the word about the Goldilocks Principle and how to apply it, we risk economic collapse, environmental collapse, geopolitical collapse, and socio-political collapse. If we successfully spread the word, we accelerate progress in every way, building the best possible future.

So, yes, we are on a mission to change the world. You are invited to join us. The choice is yours.

WHAT WE MUST DO

Once again, imagine a world where every nation has a healthy majority of people who believe in the Goldilocks Principle and understand how to apply it.

That is a world where humanity is maximizing all forms of freedom and all forms of justice at the same time.

That is a world that is constantly improving in every way—prosperity, social justice, political maturity, international harmony, and sustainability.

That ideal world is now within our grasp.

And what must we do?

We must spread the word about the Goldilocks Principle and how to apply it.

That is it. It is that simple.

And you have a role to play.

The world needs the Goldilocks Revolution, and the Goldilocks Revolution needs you.

We ask you now to do these four things:

1. Share this book and share our website (Goldilocks.org)

2. Volunteer your time (Goldilocks.org/Volunteer)

3. Donate some money (Goldilocks.org/Donate)

4. Join our weekly meetings (Goldilocks.org/WeeklyMeeting)

The change we seek does not demand extremism, just purposeful action.

By reading this book, you have already taken the first step. Now, it is time to help others discover this principle. We do not need to protest in the streets, divide ourselves further, or engage in polarizing debates. What we need is to educate ourselves and invite others to join us on this journey.

And remember, this movement is not about making everyone agree on everything. It is about inspiring a healthy majority to agree on one thing: the Goldilocks Principle.

Thank you for your help and I look forward to working alongside you as we work together to make the world a better place. Together, we can make this happen.

Join us.

Made in the USA
Middletown, DE
23 November 2024

64975518R00044